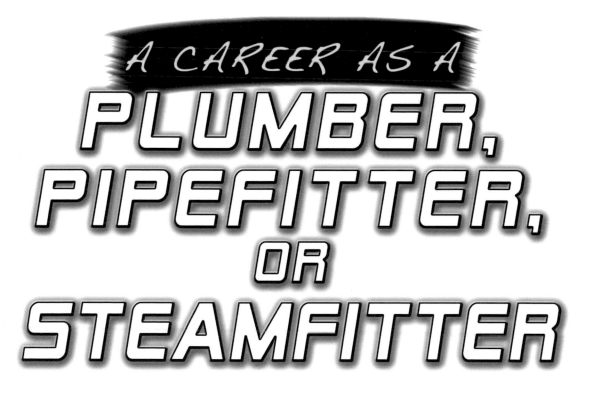

A CAREER AS A PLUMBER, PIPEFITTER, OR STEAMFITTER

A CAREER AS A
PLUMBER,
PIPEFITTER,
OR
STEAMFITTER

Rosen
YA
New York

MARY-LANE KAMBERG

For Ginger Carter

Published in 2019 by The Rosen Publishing Group, Inc.
29 East 21st Street, New York, NY 10010

First Edition

Library of Congress Cataloging-in-Publication Data

Names: Kamberg, Mary-Lane, 1948– author.
Title: A career as a plumber, pipefitter, or steamfitter / Mary-Lane Kamberg.
Description: New York : Rosen Publishing, 2019. | Series. Jobs for rebuilding America | Includes bibliographical references and index. | Audience: Grades 7–12.
Identifiers: LCCN 2017053227| ISBN 9781508179917 (library bound) | ISBN 9781508179924 (pbk.)
Subjects: LCSH: Plumbers—Juvenile literature. | Pipe fitters—Juvenile literature. | Plumbing—Vocational guidance—Juvenile literature. | Pipe fitting—Vocational guidance—Juvenile literature.
Classification: LCC TH6124 .K36 2018 | DDC 696/.1023—dc23
LC record available at https://lccn.loc.gov/2017053227

Manufactured in the United States of America

CONTENTS

O
ne Monday morning, Don got a call at his plumbing business. The water was dripping from the ceiling in the customer's garage onto his car. The homeowner thought the upstairs shower, which was located immediately above the leak, was overflowing.

"I think the shower needs to be recaulked," the caller said.

"Turn off the water," Don said. "I can get there around 1 p.m."

When Don arrived, he took a look at the shower. He went to the garage and cut a large rectangle in the sheetrock that formed the garage ceiling. He immediately knew what to do. "It's not the caulking," he said. "A part of the drain failed." Don had the part in his truck and made the repair.

Plumbers like Don are in demand. They are in demand not just by homeowners with leaky pipes but also for installations in new construction and for remodeling kitchens and bathrooms for homes and buildings alike. They are also needed for maintaining pipe systems in office buildings, industrial

Fixing leaky pipes is one of many tasks plumbers perform. They also maintain and repair pipe systems in businesses and factories and install plumbing for new construction.

sites, and dozens of different kinds of publicly and privately owned structures. Employers have reported difficulty finding workers to fill these jobs. In addition, as the United States gears up to rebuild its infrastructure, more and more workers will be needed.

Pipes and pipe systems carry water for drinking and such uses as bathing, cooking, human waste disposal, laundry, and

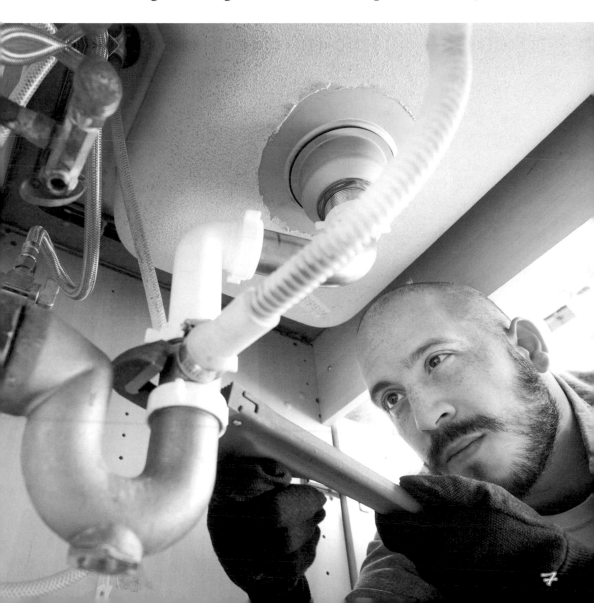

dishwashing. They also carry dirty water away. Along with water, though, pipes carry steam to make electricity by turning turbines in power plants. Pipes are also used to deliver gases used in manufacturing. Pipefitters and steamfitters share many of the same skills, as well as some specialized qualifications.

Training is available through labor unions and technical or trade schools. Requirements for becoming one of these skilled workers include classroom learning, as well as on-the-job training as a helper, apprentice, or journeyman. While learning, they work under the supervision of a master plumber with many years of experience in the field. The good news is trainees get paid while they work, unlike traditional college students who must pay tens of thousands of dollars in tuition.

At the end of journeyman training, the person can continue to work at that level or work toward the master level. Both journeymen and masters can be employed by businesses and paid according to their qualifications. But only masters can own their own businesses and/or train journeymen. Rules and requirements for licensing vary by state. And membership in a labor union may be required to work in the industry.

Because demand for skilled workers in these trades is high, and the outlook for future employment is bright, choosing a career in these fields promises good earnings and job security over time.

CHAPTER ONE

YIPES! PIPES!

*I*f you've used a drinking fountain, flushed a toilet, turned on an electric light, or enjoyed air-conditioning on a hot day, you've benefitted from the expertise of skilled workers in the trades of plumbing and fitting.

Workers like these in the construction trades are in high demand. Construction projects for homes, factories, and office buildings need the expertise of plumbers, pipefitters, and steamfitters. These skilled workers install and repair pipes that carry the water, gases, chemicals, and steam essential to modern life. Their work contributes to good hygiene and public health.

Pipe systems bring water for drinking and sanitation into and out of homes and other buildings. They also supply steam to turn the turbines that create electricity in power plants. In manufacturing, they move and remove acids, gases, and waste by-products in, out, and throughout facilities. Fire protection and sprinkler mechanisms, as well as heating, ventilation, and air-conditioning (HVAC) systems, all rely on water and other liquids and gases supplied with piping.

Bathroom remodeling may include replacing old copper pipes with new plastic ones, as well as installing new bathtubs, toilets, and sinks.

Plumbers, pipefitters, and steamfitters install and repair these systems. Sprinklerfitters install and repair fire sprinklers in businesses, factories, and apartments and other residential buildings. Gasfitters install and repair pipes that carry natural gas to ovens, as well as heating and cooling systems.

HELP ME OUT

In order to work independently as a plumber or fitter, a worker must qualify as a master plumber or master fitter. Most workers begin careers in the field through apprenticeship programs. However, some start as plumber helpers. Plumber helpers work with plumbers, pipefitters, and steamfitters doing lesser-skilled tasks than the qualified skilled workers. For example, helpers may assemble tools and equipment, hold materials or tools, take apart and remove worn out pipe, and clean work areas and equipment. Under the direction of a master plumber, a helper can cut pipe, preassemble parts, or install plumbing systems or their parts.

Apprentices learn a trade through programs run by unions and businesses. Many programs include paid on-the-job training and classroom instruction. According to the US Department of Labor, the starting pay for apprentices usually is between 30 percent and 50 percent of the rate for master plumbers, pipefitters, and steamfitters. As they gain experience, apprentices often receive pay increases. Apprenticeships typically take four to five years and around two thousand hours of workplace experience to complete. Requirements vary by state.

Once apprentices meet the requirements, they can take the state licensing exam and become licensed journeymen. Licensed journeymen must work for a master plumber. However, they don't need direct supervision for most tasks. They can work on both small and large projects. In most states, a journeyman can become a master after one year's experience. However, some states require more time and expertise to earn a license.

Apprentices learn on the job under the supervision of a qualified plumber. An apprenticeship can last four to five years, including classroom training.

ON THE JOB

Plumbers and fitters perform a wide variety of duties. They read blueprints and choose materials and equipment for each job. They must follow state and local building codes. Building codes are regulations or ordinances enacted and enforced by state and local governments. They establish minimum standards to ensure structural safety of homes and other buildings.

WORLD TOILET DAY?

In the Western world, indoor plumbing and flush toilets are so common that you might think the idea of World Toilet Day is somebody's idea of a joke. However, the lack of such facilities in developing countries isn't funny at all.

According to the World Toilet Day website, 4.5 billion people worldwide live without a home toilet. And, only 20 percent of all wastewater is treated before it flows back into rivers and other water bodies. The rest is raw sewage. When people use contaminated water for drinking and other uses, they risk coming down with such illnesses as cholera, dysentery, typhoid, and polio, according to the World Health Organization. This has resulted in a global sanitation crisis.

Besides spreading disease, it also affects nations' economies. Loss of productivity due to illnesses spread by untreated water is estimated to cost as much as 5 percent of some countries' gross domestic product, again according to the World Toilet Day website. That's why, in 2013, the United Nations General Assembly declared November 19 as World Toilet Day. The day is dedicated to raising awareness of this threat to human health. Its goal is to ensure that everyone has access to a safe household toilet by 2030.

These workers install pipes and connect them with fittings. Fittings include joints, couplings, elbows, tees, or other parts to join pipes together. Plumbers and fitters also inspect installed pipelines and perform pressure tests to make sure the pipe systems are airtight or watertight. Duties also include troubleshooting systems that aren't working properly and replacing worn parts.

In the course of their work, plumbers and fitters also measure pipe and use saws or pipe cutters to cut and bend it. They may cut holes in walls, floors, and ceilings or hang supports from ceilings to hold pipe in place. Workers with advanced skills supervise apprentices and helpers.

YOUNG AND OLD

As important as the skilled trades of plumbing and fitting are, experts see a shortage of qualified workers that will worsen in the near future. However, persuading them to pursue these careers isn't easy.

For one thing, few are attracted to the idea of unstopping toilets, crawling around in basements, and other icky jobs. Plumbers and fitters may need to perform some of those tasks. However, they also work on new construction of residential and office buildings. Workers in these trades may be involved in kitchen and bathroom renovations and in replacing water heaters and dishwashers.

It's also likely that young people have not been encouraged to consider these jobs. They may not realize that the pay and benefits in this industry are above average compared to all

Licensed master plumbers can own their own businesses. As their enterprises grow, they may hire helpers, apprentices, journeymen, or even fellow master plumbers to help them out.

occupations. According to the US Bureau of Labor Statistics, master plumbers and fitters earn about 30 percent more than the median average for all occupations. The median average is the point where 50 percent of workers earn more and 50 percent earn less.

The emphasis on STEM (science, technology, engineering, and math) education in grades kindergarten through twelve may spur interest among students who may prefer careers in skilled trades.

WOMEN'S WORK

Another potential source for future plumbers and fitters is among women. The first American woman to hold a master plumber's license was Lillian Ann Baumbach of Arlington, Virginia, in 1951. However, these careers have traditionally been dominated by men. According to the US Department of Labor, only 1.1 percent of the more than a half million plumbers, pipe layers, pipefitters, and steamfitters in the United States in 2010 were women.

Some of the same drawbacks for young workers also exist for women of all ages. Plumbing and fitting are considered get-your-hands-dirty careers. And, until PVC (polyvinyl chloride) piping was invented around the time of World War II, plumbers and fitters needed considerable strength to carry heavy pipes and parts. However, today's use of the relatively lightweight PVC, ABS (acrylonitrile butadiene styrene), and DWV (drain-waste-vent) PVC pipes and products makes physical strength a less important factor for these workers. (However, both men and women do need strength to perform the jobs.)

In addition, some women who have entered the field report such barriers as discrimination and reluctance by experienced male workers to share knowledge. Others describe lack of adequate bathrooms for women on construction sites. Jobs in the industry are competitive, and some women say they aren't offered as many hours as their male counterparts. However, improved outreach to women of all ages could result in more women entering the trades.

CHAPTER TWO

GO WITH THE FLOW

E very day is different for working plumbers. They're qualified to perform a wide variety of tasks. But, they may not know which jobs they'll be asked to perform—or when or where they will be doing them. Some workers, called "wet only" plumbers, work on pipes for bathrooms and radiators. Others, known as "gas only" plumbers, work in factories and perform other industrial work that focuses on moving air and other gases through pipe systems.

Plumbers work in both residences and commercial buildings. Those who work in the residential side of the industry install a wide variety of pipe systems. These include water, drainage, and gas pipes in homes, as well as small water lines that lead to refrigerators with icemakers and drinking water dispensers. Plumbers install such fixtures as bathtubs, showers, sinks, and toilets for both new construction and remodeling projects. They may also install dishwashers, garbage disposals, or water heaters. Repairing and replacing leaking pipes is also a big part of their job.

DIRTY WORK

Plumbers do handle such dirty work as unclogging pipes for sinks, toilets, and other drains and maintaining septic systems. A septic system is a method used to treat and dispose of human

Some plumbers clean, maintain, and repair septic systems, which are used to treat and dispose of human sanitary waste in mostly rural areas not connected to central sewer systems.

sanitary waste. These systems are often installed in rural areas that do not have access to city sewers. According to Mr. Rooter .com, about one-fourth of American households use individual septic systems.

In a septic system, a watertight underground tank holds the waste while anaerobic bacteria decompose it. Anaerobic bacteria grow without the need for oxygen. Once the material decomposes, tank lines distribute the liquid waste into a drain field of underground soil. There, layers of rock and soil filter out the bacteria and clean the water before it seeps into the groundwater. Groundwater is water that starts as rain or snowmelt. It seeps beneath Earth's surface and collects in spaces between rock. Groundwater is the source for wells and springs.

Plumbers help maintain these systems. They inspect connections inside the house by flushing toilets and running water in sinks, washing machines, and other appliances. They also inspect the sludge levels in the septic tank and periodically pump out the solid waste left in it. They look for cracks in the tank and signs that the drainfield is working properly.

SKILLS AND TALENTS

To perform their tasks, plumbers need good communication skills. They must listen and understand others' spoken and written speech. They must also be able to convey ideas and information through speech and writing. They're expected to share information with supervisors, coworkers, and subordinates by telephone, in written form, via email, and in person.

Plumbers need good reasoning skills using both deductive and inductive reasoning. Deductive reasoning applies general rules to specific situations. Inductive reasoning creates general rules by combining pieces of information. Another important skill is the ability to recognize a problem or tell if something is likely to go wrong.

The ability to visualize the result of moving or rearranging items helps plumbers come up with several ideas for solving problems, as does arranging tasks in an order or pattern that

A clogged sink or toilet is one of many everyday, common issues plumbers deal with. Another is a bathtub that refuses to drain.

makes sense for the job. Finally, plumbers must concentrate on the same job for long periods without becoming distracted.

Other necessary skills include the ability to review blueprints and understand building codes. Plumbers inspect structures to determine needed supplies and equipment. They also estimate time, material, and labor costs for each project and decide the order work will be done in. The must keep records of the jobs they perform.

ECO-FRIENDLY PLUMBING

Because of environmental concerns, many plumbers recommend and install eco-friendly equipment and alternative water sources to save fresh water and lower water and energy costs. Environmentally friendly equipment includes flow restrictors, dual flush toilets, pressure-assisted flush toilets, and tankless water heaters.

Flow restrictors limit the amount of water that comes out of a faucet or showerhead to reduce the amount of water needed for showers or dishwashing. Dual flush toilets offer two flush options. One is for liquid waste, which requires less water to dispose of than solid waste, which needs a full tank of water to clear. Pressure-assisted flush toilets use compressed air or a water pump to boost flushing power. Standard toilets that use gravity to empty the water tank typically use 1.6 gallons (6 liters) of water per flush. Pressure-assisted toilets use 1.1 to 1.4 gallons (4.2 to 5.3 liters). According to the US Environmental Protection Agency, a family of four can annually save several thousand gallons of water.

LET'S GET PHYSICAL

Plumbers work with their hands. They also use their entire bodies. They must be physically fit enough to perform many of the tasks required of them. They walk, stoop, balance, and climb, as well as handle, position, and move materials. They need the following abilities:

- **Hands and fingers.** Plumbers need the ability to move fingers quickly and precisely. And they need the same skill to use one or both hands to hold, control, or assemble objects. They must be able to keep hands and arms steady when they hold an object in a set position.
- **Arms and legs.** These workers need good coordination of both arms, both legs, or one of each when they sit, stand, or lie down.
- **Torso.** Plumbers need flexibility so they can bend, stretch, twist, and reach. They need good balance. And they need strong abdominal and lower back muscles to work for a long time without getting tired. Of course, they also need strength to lift, push, pull, or carry objects.
- **Eyesight.** Plumbers need good general (or corrected) eyesight for both near and far vision.

Standard water heaters heat and store water until it's needed. However, tankless water heaters (also known as flash, demand, or instantaneous water heaters) wait to heat the water until it's needed. Tankless water heaters run on propane, natural gas, or electricity.

Alternative water sources include rainwater harvesting systems and gray water reuse systems. Rainwater harvesting systems collect rainwater in special tanks where it is filtered and saved for later use at the same site. These systems reduce reliance on water storage dams, minimize the risk of overloading storm water systems in neighborhoods, and reduce water bills.

Gray water reuse systems collect and treat household wastewater from showers, bathtubs, laundry, and sinks. Treated water can be recycled for doing laundry, flushing toilets, and watering plants, lawns, and landscaping.

DISASTER RELIEF

Plumbers are often on call to fix emergency situations like leaking pipes. Extreme cold can result in frozen pipes. And frozen pipes can burst, spewing water everywhere. Extreme heat can cause plumbing and heating systems to break down. If a homeowner's pipes leak, he or she can't wait until the next day for help. Plumbers must be available at all hours, day or night. (In larger companies, plumbers take turns being on call. In smaller companies, everyone must be available all the time.)

Some companies specialize in emergency situations. For example, the Emergency Plumbing Squad offers the availability

Earthquakes and other disasters that affect large areas often require emergency workers to repair or replace damaged pipe systems. Wherever large relief and repair efforts are happening, you will find plumbers and fitters.

of master plumbers twenty-four hours a day. The company has locations in Manhattan, Brooklyn, Queens, and the Bronx in New York, as well as in Denver, Colorado, and Birmingham, Alabama.

Sometimes emergencies affect more than one household. A tornado, hurricane, earthquake, or other natural disaster can cause plumbing problems over a wide area. Ruptured pipes and other pipe system failures can occur. After catastrophes, plumbers are needed to work long, hard hours to restore their communities.

CHAPTER THREE

IT'S ONLY FITTING

*P*ipefitters and steamfitters are two of many specialties included in the plumbing industry. Pipefitters perform plumbing jobs on large, industrial projects. Steamfitters work on high-pressure systems that pipe water, steam, or compressed air for various uses.

Pipefitters and steamfitters perform many of the same tasks as plumbers. Sometimes simply called "fitters," they assemble, install, and maintain pipe systems. These pipes often carry acids, gases, liquids, and chemicals for industrial use. These pipe systems are also used for lubrication and heating, ventilation, and air-conditioning in such settings as power plants, factories, and office buildings. This work includes installing the large water lines that bring water into the structures, as well as underground storm and sanitary pipe systems.

Fitters connect pipe sections using a variety of parts, materials, and methods. They use couplings, clamps, screws, and bolts. Steel pipe is often screwed together. Pipes made of other materials are joined using cement, plastic solvent, or caulking. Other methods include soldering, brazing, or welding parts together. For example, fitters connect copper pipe using solder. Solder is an alloy—usually of tin and lead—that melts at low temperatures. Soldering uses the melted alloy to connect pipe

Fitters install, maintain, and repair large pipe systems, such as those used to discharge treated liquid waste into a river.

without heating it to the melting point. Brazing is soldering that uses an alloy of copper and zinc at a high temperature. For small pipes, fitters may use welding. Welding joins metals together by heating them to the melting point using a blowtorch or other tool. The parts are then further joined by pressing or hammering them.

PIPING HOT

Factories, college campuses, and natural-gas power plants need pipe systems that move steam under high pressure to generate heat and electricity. Like all fitters, steamfitters create, assemble, maintain, and repair pipe systems. In addition to factories, schools, and power plants, they work in homes, hospitals, and wastewater treatment plants and on industrial projects and new construction.

Skilled female craftsmen are underrepresented in the building trades. However, as demand for these workers increases, women are beginning to get more work as plumbers and fitters.

Steamfitters work at all stages of piping projects. They may create sketches of a system or read and interpret blueprints and pipe specifications. Using tools and observation, they measure pipe width and length and recognize different types of pipe. Holes might have to be cut in walls to insert pipes. These workers must also use pipe testing equipment to look for leaks. Steamfitters work with carbon, stainless steel, and alloy metals and shape them to fit using bending or welding.

Steamfitters are on their feet most of the workday. The pipes they work with are found in large and small places both indoors and outdoors. These workers must be able to climb high walls and crawl into tight spaces. They also need strength and endurance to carry heavy items. Pipes can break any time. So, steamfitters whose responsibilities include maintenance of pipe systems are always on call to make repairs. Many of them have to be ready nights, weekends, and holidays for urgent or emergency situations that may arise.

OTHER SPECIALTIES

Aside from pipefitters and steamfitters, some of the more common specialties in the plumbing industry are gasfitters, sprinklerfitters, and HVAC mechanical service pipefitters.

(CONTINUED ON THE NEXT PAGE)

29

(CONTINUED FROM THE PREVIOUS PAGE)

- Gasfitters work on pipe systems related to the use of natural gas, as well as other gases. They install, maintain, and repair systems that carry natural gas to stoves, furnaces, and water heaters. They also install, remove, and repair the appliances themselves, as well as such related equipment as gas meters, valves, burners, and regulators. This specialty includes work on natural gas and propane appliances in boats, ships, motorhomes, and trains. It also involves pipes that provide oxygen to hospital patients.

- Sprinklerfitters design, install, inspect, certify, and repair fire sprinkler systems in businesses, factories, and residential buildings. Also called fire suppression systems, these sprinklers most often use water. However, they may contain air, antifreeze, gas, chemicals, or a mixture that produces fire retardant foam. The systems must comply with fire codes. Sprinklerfitters work with pipes and tubing made of plastic, copper, steel, and iron. These workers must maintain good physical fitness because the job includes heavy lifting.

- HVAC mechanical service pipefitters install, maintain, and repair mechanical systems for heating, cooling, and refrigeration. They work in houses, office buildings, warehouses, grocery stores, restaurants, ice rinks, hospitals, oil refineries, nuclear power plants, steel mills, and factories. Most of the systems they work on are found outdoors. The pipes they work on carry chilled water, hot water, and lubricants for industrial production and other uses. Some HVAC fitters provide Earth-friendly geothermal heating and cooling systems. These systems use a heat pump, liquid, and ductwork to conduct heat from belowground to a house or building in winter and carry heat in and around the structure for cooling in summer.

MIND AND BODY

Fitters need the same physical fitness traits that plumbers need. In addition, fitters need to be able to coordinate their entire body—arms, legs, and torso—when they are in motion. They also need quick reaction time so they can use the hand, foot, or finger to answer when such signals as sounds, lights, or pictures appear. Along with good general (or corrected) eyesight, fitters need good depth perception so they can tell which objects are closer or farther from each other. Fitters also need good hearing, including being able to focus on a single sound among other distracting ones in often noisy environments.

Fitters also need to process information by placing it in categories, and tabulating or verifying data. They must come up with original ways to deal with situations and solve problems. And they need the ability to evaluate information for good decision making.

PEOPLE TO PEOPLE

Most independent residential plumbers work alone. Fitters, on the other hand, often work with others. There may be other fitters on the same project. Other construction tradesmen, such as carpenters, electricians, ironworkers, and laborers, will also be present. Communication and people skills are important in this collaborative environment.

They need to be able to form working relationships and maintain them over time. They may be called upon to coordinate other workers so they work well together, as well as stay out of each other's way. Part of a skilled worker's job is to train those with fewer skills. The skilled worker must identify the other workers' educational needs, help them brush up on their skills, teach them new ones, or recommend formal training programs. Working with others may also entail rating the quality of the work that others perform.

WORKING HARD

Fitters participate in the entire process of pipe systems, starting with gathering and evaluating information about the project.

Pipefitters and steamfitters need strength to carry heavy pipes and agility to climb high walls and crawl into tight spaces both indoors and outdoors.

This information includes the result of inspections of the work site itself, looking for holes or obstacles that could affect the work. They plan the work and the order in which it will be completed in compliance with building codes.

Fitters' responsibilities may include plans for the layout of the pipe system, including drawings and detailed instructions for making, assembling, modifying, maintaining, or using the system. They choose pipe types and sizes. And they measure and mark pipes for cutting and cut them. Their job may include connecting pipes by welding, brazing, cementing, soldering, or threading. Threading is a way of assembling pipe systems using screw ends.

They may install automatic controls to regulate pipe systems. Troubleshooting duties include inspecting and testing pipelines. Once the cause of a problem is determined, fitters may clean, modify, remove, or replace parts or equipment. Perhaps most important, fitters must stay up-to-date and take advantage of new technical advances in their work.

CHAPTER FOUR

PLANNING AHEAD

*T*o work in the skilled trades of plumbing and fitting, you must be at least eighteen years old and have a high school diploma or equivalent. But you don't have to wait until then to start preparing for these careers. You can start learning necessary information and skills while you're still in high school.

Doing coursework in STEM classes, including math, engineering, information technology, and the sciences, is a way to develop sharp technical skills that future plumbers and fitters will need to rely on.

Your basic education should include mathematics, English language skills, engineering, science, business, and information technology as well as mechanical knowledge of machines and tools. Don't forget physical education classes or extracurricular and after-school sports or training to build strength and conditioning.

Plumbers and fitters use arithmetic, algebra, geometry, calculus, and statistics. So take as many math classes as you can. Unions and employers look for candidates with strong math skills, particularly in algebra and geometry. They may request ACT math scores. You'll also need a working knowledge of the metric system.

Written and oral communication also are critical in these trades. Most websites and organizations, like unions, that advertise job openings require knowledge of the English language. Try to make sure you have a basic and adequate comprehension of spelling, grammar, and the rules of composition. English language and composition classes cover these topics. So do classes in speech, drama, and debate.

Students should become familiar with engineering, science, and technology and how they apply to the design and production of goods and services. Look for engineering classes that cover industrial and production technology for construction and manufacturing. If possible, take a drafting class either in high school or through a community college or technical school. Science classes should include physics and chemistry. Ask around also to see if your school or school district offers classes in public safety and security.

BUSINESS AS USUAL

Many workers in the construction trades will also want to get an overall view of how businesses work. Many of them want to start their own businesses after they achieve master plumber or master fitter status and get some years of experience under their belts. Such high school classes as introductory business, accounting, entrepreneurship, marketing, and business law cover the basics. If you cannot fit in business courses in high school, or your school does not offer them, you can try to take them at a community college. Many districts have arrangements with

Competence in a wide variety of computer software is necessary for many jobs, and nowadays a laptop is as common a tool in a plumber's repetoire as a wrench.

local community colleges and other institutions for students to try these out and use them for high school and college credit.

Information technology is as important in skilled trades as in other careers. Students must be familiar with software for internet browsers, email, word processing, and spreadsheets through such programs as Microsoft Office. For instance, two good spreadsheet programs are Microsoft Excel and Piping Office. Knowing how to use accounting, database, and facilities management software is another plus.

Advanced software also is helpful. Computer aided design (CAD) software like AEC Design Group CADPIPE and ViziFlow assist plumbers and fitters. So do such analytical or scientific software as Bentley Systems AutoPIPE, COADE CAESAR II, Pipepro Pipefitting, and Watter Hammer Software Hytran. Also look for project management software that helps estimate construction costs for pipe systems.

CAREER SKILLS

SkillsUSA is a national association that helps middle school, high school, and college students get ready for careers in the construction trades and other industries. Its goal is to ensure that the United States has a skilled workforce. Members include students, teachers, and industry representatives who help students become world-class workers.

Founded in 1965, SkillsUSA has served more than 12.5 million members according to its website. Current membership includes more than 335,000 students and advisers in 18,000 chapters in fifty-two states and territories. Members work together to develop personal, workplace, and technical skills. Its vision is "to produce the most highly skilled workforce in the world." More than six hundred businesses and labor and industry organizations contribute time and money to SkillsUSA via volunteers and financial aid.

The association's programs include local, state, and national opportunities for students to learn and practice personal, workplace, and technical skills. SkillsUSA Championships are national technical competitions in one hundred occupational and leadership skill areas.

In addition, the association provides resources for teachers and students, including a Chapter Excellence Program that honors local branches. Another program seeks to help students develop skills, attitudes, and values that give them an edge over competing applicants. There is also an OSHA (Occupational Safety and Health Administration) safety-training program and one that encourages students to mentor younger students interested in the trades. The US Department of Education has recognized SkillsUSA as a successful model of employer-driven youth development training.

HONING SOCIAL SKILLS

Middle school and high school are periods of students' lives when they should be learning the kinds of people skills they'll need in the future—whether for work, academia, or their personal lives. Among these skills are the ability to build relationships and direct, follow, and teach others. Experience with classroom projects as well as extracurricular activities builds these abilities.

Participating in theatrical performances, for example, gives students a chance to work together as well as make such individual contributions as acting, creating sets, and coordinating props. As everyone works together to achieve a common goal, each learns the value of his or her own and others' roles. Team sports offer the same kinds of opportunities. Teammates learn to follow instructions from coaches and team captains. Athletes also get chances to lead their peers by example. Sharing tips about athletic techniques gives the experience for teaching work skills to fellow workers.

HANDS-ON LEARNING

Career and technical education classes are especially good for those who plan to work in the construction trades. These programs involve both learning and practicing some of the tasks involved in the building careers. You can learn to use tools and machines and also learn about their design, maintenance, and repair.

ARE YOU READY FOR A CAREER IN THE PLUMBING INDUSTRY?

Do you have what it takes for a career as a plumber or fitter? In addition to academic knowledge and practical hands-on skills, you'll need to develop these abilities:

- **Active listening.** Can you give undivided attention when someone is speaking? Do you understand the person's main points? Do you ask appropriate questions without interrupting?
- **Critical thinking.** Can you identify strengths and weaknesses of potential solutions to problems? Do you use logic and reasoning when you approach problems?
- **Decision-making.** Do you use cost-benefit analysis when picking a course of action to take?
- **Complex problem-solving.** When faced with complex problems, do you seek additional information in order to develop, compare, or solve them?
- **Active learning.** As you learn new information, can you incorporate it into your problem-solving and decision-making?
- **Time management.** Do you set priorities to make the best use of your time?

Opportunities for hands-on learning help prepare students for careers in the trades. While not too many high schools have extensive programs that prepare students just for plumbing, other skills can be built in related technical fields.

For example, the Olathe School District in Kansas offers a two-year career and technical education program for students interested in construction trades. The first year consists of classes in residential carpentry, remodeling, business maintenance, cabinet making and furniture design, and plumbing technology. The second year's program includes advanced residential carpentry and advanced cabinet making and furniture design as well as electrical and security systems and HVAC and plumbing systems.

Students complete a large construction project as part of the program. The project may be building a house, another large construction project, or a community service project. They measure objects and perform math calculations. They also work with blueprints, materials lists, tools, and equipment. They learn how to maintain and repair a home and learn about building codes and requirements for building permits. Students are introduced to such career choices as working for commercial contractors and home builders in construction, remodeling, and maintenance work.

These kinds of programs give students a chance to work with some of the tools they'll need. Plumbers and fitters use a variety of hand tools, power tools, and machines. For example, they use simple tools like rulers and levels to mark positions of connections, obstacles, or other features of a pipe system. They use pipe cutters, pipe-threading machines, or pipe-bending machines to cut or bend pipe to the right shape and length. They read pressure gauges to find leaks. They also may use crescent wrenches, pipe wrenches, and hacksaws as well as cutting or welding torches. These are just a few of the tools and machines plumbers must know how to use.

CHAPTER FIVE

STEP BY STEP

*A*fter you finish high school, it's time for more learning. You'll need classroom work, as well as experience, over a period of four to five years. The most common way to gain this knowledge and practical application is through an apprenticeship in plumbing or fitting. Apprenticeships are offered through a local union affiliated with such organizations as the Plumbing-Heating-Cooling Contractors Association and the United Association Union of Plumbers, Fitters, Welders, and HVAC Service Techs. Some businesses also offer specific task-oriented training.

Apprentices qualify for licenses simply by working under the direct supervision of a licensed plumber or instructors at an approved trade or technical school. During the apprentice period, trainees must log 1,700 to 2,000 hours of on-the-job experience per year under the supervision of a journeyman or master plumber or fitter. Apprentices learn about plumbing tools and machines. They'll also gain experience with installing, maintaining, and repairing pipe systems and their components. Apprentices also annually need about 250 hours of theoretical and technical classroom instruction.

To qualify for an apprenticeship, you'll need a high school diploma (preferred) or a GED (general equivalency diploma). You must be eighteen years of age and have a valid driver's

Plumbers and fitters benefit greatly from having more skilled and senior members of their profession guide them through the hands-on training that apprenticeships are so good at providing.

license with a clean driving record. In some states, you must also pass a mandatory drug test and a criminal background check.

Some apprenticeships require a math or an aptitude test. The aptitude test may include math, reading comprehension, and general plumbing knowledge. Before registering for the test, ask for a practice test or study guide you can use to prepare for it. Some states require apprentices to be licensed before they begin work. Where required, these licenses are granted by individual state boards.

WHAT IS THE UNIFORM PLUMBING CODE?

The Uniform Plumbing Code keeps the quality of plumbing consistent nationwide. The code includes rules for installation and maintenance of plumbing fixtures, fixture fittings, water heaters, sanitary drainage, and storm drainage as well as fire protection, gray water systems, and plumbing for health care facilities.

The Uniform Plumbing Code grew out of a problem recognized by building inspectors in Los Angeles, California, in 1926. At the time, no official standards covered plumbing installation or maintenance. Inspectors became frustrated by the lack of consistency in the pipe systems they were responsible for. The inspectors teamed with plumbers associations to develop the first uniform plumbing code for their area. It improved quality in the plumbing industry.

In 1945, the Western Plumbing Association adopted the code and applied it to the entire United States. The International Association of Plumbing and Mechanical Officials (IAPMO) updates the code twice a year on average, according to results of scientific studies and analysis.

EDGING OUT THE COMPETITION

Applying for an apprenticeship is highly competitive. It's not uncommon for hundreds of applicants to try for just a few openings. Some applicants first gain experience by working as a plumber helper. Plumber helpers make relatively low wages as they assist plumbers on jobs. Helpers observe licensed tradesmen in action and learn from them. One place to find training for helpers is through the Home Builders Institute.

In addition to technical skills, plumbers need such communication skills as active listening and the ability to explain needed repairs.

It provides preapprenticeship training for plumbing and seven other construction trades through its Pre-Apprenticeship Certificate Training (PACT) program.

You can also take some of your state's required classroom training before applying for an apprenticeship. Look for such classes as plumbing fundamentals, blueprint reading, drafting, piping systems, pipe system design, plumbing codes and regulations, safety issues, and classes in math, chemistry, and physics. Students interested in pipefitting and steamfitting may take welding courses.

You'll find these classes at community colleges and vocational, trade, or technical schools. Some offer online or correspondence programs. Find schools near you by entering "plumbing and fitting trade schools" and your city, state, or zip code into your search engine. Before enrolling, ensure the schools are accredited and offer the kinds of classes you need. Also look for reviews by former students, and do research to make sure schools really prepare students with the skills that employers will want. Avoid schools with suspicious websites or ones that charge students money with little return. These are sometimes known as "diploma mills."

You can gain experience in the construction trades by volunteering for such projects as the Low Income Housing Institute or Habitat for Humanity. The Low Income House Institute uses volunteers to build tiny houses for the homeless in the Seattle, Washington, area. Habitat for Humanity builds affordable houses for people who need adequate shelter. Volunteers work alongside potential homeowners who contribute "sweat equity," which means contributing their physical work to the value of their home. According to its

Building houses for organizations like Habitat for Humanity is a good way to gain experience before apprenticeships. Here, actors (*left to right*) Larenz Tate, Glynn Turman, and Donis Leonard, Jr. are shown after a day working for the charity.

website, Habitat for Humanity has served nearly ten million people in 1,400 American communities and seventy countries.

LOOKING GOOD ON PAPER

By taking classes before seeking an apprenticeship, you'll stand out above others who have not completed them. You will also decrease the number of classroom hours you'll need later. These schools often help students find apprenticeships with labor unions, plumbing companies, or individual master plumbers.

You'll need to complete a written application. It's a good idea to attach a résumé. A résumé is a document that summarizes your education, qualifications, and personal and professional experience. Each item should contribute to a picture of you as the best possible candidate.

Your résumé should include everything related to the trade. Be specific. List applicable classes you have taken in high school, community college, or trade or technical school, with special emphasis on math, science, and drafting. List computer software you have proficiency with. Include extracurricular and volunteer activities that contribute to the skills plumbers and fitters need.

If you worked on a construction project as part of a high school program or worked as a plumber helper, list the specific ways you contributed to the project. Did you help install the bathroom sink, bend pipe to fit, or observe pressure tests? If you've helped with maintenance or repair of pipes in your own home, describe what you did.

List all past employment and highlight such experiences as customer service, working with tools, and anything that translates into your ability to perform plumbers' and fitters' duties. Did you plan work schedules? Direct or train fellow employees? Did you work with your hands in a mechanical capacity? Did you work without direct supervision? Can you maintain accurate records and daily activity reports? What plumbing tools have you used? List them. Keep in mind that the information on a résumé must be true and accurate. Many employers fire workers who lie on their résumés, even if they're doing a good job.

Ask a teacher or other trusted adult to help you create a professional résumé to use when applying for an apprenticeship.

While apprenticeships at local unions are the first choice for many aspiring plumbers, applicants who aren't accepted for union programs can still find the training they need. You can contact plumbing businesses and individual master plumbers to seek a position. Before starting an apprenticeship, get a list of state and local requirements for the journeyman exam. If possible, order practice tests. That way you'll have an idea of the things you need to learn during this period of training. You'll be prepared for the journeyman exam at the completion of your apprenticeship.

CHAPTER SIX

STEPPING UP

Once you complete your state's apprenticeship requirements, you will earn a certificate of apprenticeship. However, in many states, you must complete at least one more step before you can work independently. Most states and localities require plumbers to be licensed. Some states require licenses for pipefitters and special licenses for those who work on gas lines.

In most states, you'll need a journey-level license, which means you must pass an exam. It will be worth it. You'll be qualified for more jobs at higher pay as long as you work for a licensed master plumber. A journeyman plumber can do most plumbing tasks without direct supervision, except for creating piping designs and sizing pipes.

Hopefully, you have learned and gained experience in the areas the state tests on. It's still a good idea to prepare for the journeyman exam. Seek out study guides and sample tests. Many are available online. Enter "sample journeyman plumber exam" or "sample journeyman pipefitter exam" in your web browser. Be sure the materials you study from include the most recent building codes for your state. Also, review the most recent local codes for your area. If you know other apprentices who are taking the test, get together and practice asking and answering questions.

You can prepare for the journeyman exam by reviewing your state's current building codes and completing online practice tests.

For the best chance of success, find out what you can and cannot bring into the testing center. (Sometimes parts of the test are open book.) Stop studying the day before the test to give yourself a chance to relax and let the information you already know settle in. Consider a practice run from your home to the testing center to determine how much travel time you'll need and whether there are any potential roadblocks, construction, or other obstacles. Get plenty of sleep the night before. Plan to arrive for the exam thirty minutes early.

IS THIS ON THE TEST?

The journey-level exams for plumbers and fitters determine whether you've learned what you need to know. For more information, check with your state's licensing board. The exams may include the sections outlined on the following page.

Plumbers must learn how to interpret and use detailed plumbing diagrams showing intake lines, hot and cold water pipes, plumbing fixtures, appliances, and sewage and ventilation pipes.

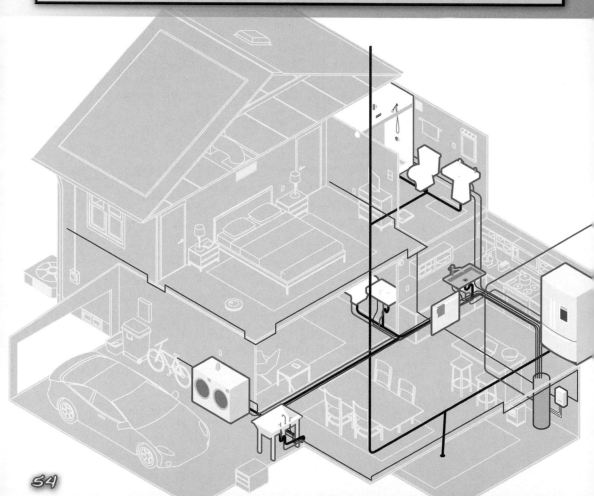

PLUMBER'S EXAM

- Administrative policies and procedures
- General regulations
- Fixtures
- Water heaters
- Water supply and distribution
- Sanitary drainage systems
- Indirect and special wastes
- Vents and venting
- Traps, clean-outs, and interceptors
- Recycling gray water
- Special piping and storage systems

PIPEFITTER'S EXAM

The journey-level pipefitter exam is offered through the National Inspection Testing Certification (NITC). It consists of one hundred multiple-choice questions. Topics include general pipefitting knowledge, as well as the following:

- Pipefitting mathematics
- Welding
- Rigging
- Air-conditioning refrigeration and hydronics. (Hydronics is a type of heating or cooling technology that transfers heat using water, vapor, or other fluid in a closed pipe system.)
- State and national codes
- Ethical standards

SAMPLE PLUMBER'S EXAM QUESTIONS

Actual test questions are not published before the test. However, here are some typical samples:

1. You know how to install a brass device with slip nuts and washers as part of a tub waste and overflow installation. What else do you need to know in order to correctly complete the job?
   a. The waste-and-overflow installation must be accessible.
   b. The connection requires an access panel.
   c. The assembly must be accessible.
   d. You cannot use nylon washers under the slip nuts.

2. A lavatory drain must have a diameter of at least _____.
   a. 1.25 inches
   b. 1.5 inches
   c. 2 inches
   d. 2.5 inches.

3. As part of a remodeling job, you will replace an existing toilet, shower, and water heater in the same places where the old ones exist. Which of these need a plumbing permit and code inspection?
   a. Toilet
   b. Shower
   c. Water heater
   d. All of the above

4. Gray water for recycling can be collected from which of the following?
   a. Clothes washers
   b. Bathtubs and showers
   c. Sinks
   d. All of the above

5. True or false: Island vents are never allowed for installation on sinks and lavatories.

Source: Tests.com

MASTERS OF THE TRADE

After a year or so as a journeyman, you'll be ready to take the master-level licensing exam. Many plumbers, pipefitters, and steamfitters choose to remain at the journey level. Increased income is the main reason to achieve the master level. According to Salary.com, master plumbers earn about 30 percent more than journeymen.

As a master plumber, if you're an employee of a plumbing company, you'll be among the highest paid workers. A master plumber license shows that you have advanced installation, maintenance, and repair skills. But you'll also be able to start your own business as a full-service plumbing company contractor. According to the US Bureau of Labor Statistics, about 10 percent of plumbers, pipefitters, and steamfitters were self-employed in 2014.

As a master plumber, you expand the list of jobs you can do. For example, on some construction jobs master plumbers help develop blueprints that show where pipes and fixtures are to be located. Their responsibilities may also include ensuring the project meets building codes, stays within budget, and coordinates with placement of electric wires or other features. Some of these are created using building information modeling (BIM) software. So being able to use this technology increases job prospects. Master plumbers also may evaluate, coordinate, and delegate work orders. They may meet with potential customers to review plumbing issues.

Like the journeyman-level exam, the master-level test varies by state. It usually consists of multiple-choice and true/false questions. The test isn't easy. However, remember that you have gained practical knowledge and experience in your apprenticeship and journeyman work. Again, look for practice tests online. Study building codes.

Consider installing a study guide app on your mobile phone so you can review information anywhere, any time. For example, Edu Leaders Inc. offers a Master Plumber Exam Prep app that includes flashcards, a matching game, and true/false and multiple-choice questions. You can also track your learning progress.

CHAPTER SEVEN

PIPE DREAMS

So how do you find a job and get ahead in the plumbing, pipefitting, and steamfitting industry? In addition to knowledge and practical skills, you'll need to develop personal qualities to increase your chances for success. A reputation for reliability, responsibility, and dependability goes a long way. So do being honest and ethical.

Along with other indoor and outdoor jobs, pipefitters may be involved in the installation of precast, U-shaped concrete drains at construction sites.

Cooperation and pleasant interaction with coworkers are musts. When necessary, you'll need to demonstrate strong leadership.

You will also want to show attention to detail and a willingness to take on new challenges. You'll need creativity, persistence, and logic. And you'll have to be able to accept criticism and make appropriate changes when necessary. Perhaps one of the most important traits of all is the ability to depend on yourself to get jobs done with little or no supervision.

GETTING A JOB

Good places to start looking for a job as a plumber, pipefitter, or steamfitter are the places where you did your training as an apprentice or journeyman. Networking is another good way. Contact tradesmen you worked with on previous jobs. Ask if they know anyone who is hiring. Knowing someone is a tried-and-true way to find jobs in all occupations.

You can also find job listings on union job banks and websites. For example, Steamfitters and Plumbers Local Union 464 in Omaha, Nebraska, posts job openings online. So do state government job centers, universities, and individual businesses. They list specific requirements for each job, as well as how to apply.

The internet is loaded with websites that list job openings. Some are national. Some let you enter your zip code or state to narrow your search. Check out these examples:

- Indeed.com
- DiversityJobs.com

- CareerBuilder.com
- US.jobs
- Monster.com
- Adzuna.com
- HBICareers.silkroad.com

OPEN OR CLOSED?

Depending on your state's labor laws, you may find a job in an open shop, agency shop, closed shop, or union shop. These designations apply to the employer's relationship with labor unions. A labor union is an organization of wage earners or salaried employees in a particular trade. The union seeks to protect and further such members' issues as wages, benefits, and working conditions.

An open shop, sometimes called a merit shop, is a company that is free to hire both members and nonmembers. Some open shops recognize the union as its only negotiating agent. An agency shop is an employer that uses the union as a bargaining agent. In an agency shop, all employees pay dues to the union even if they are not union members. An employer of a closed shop hires only union members in good standing. A union shop is an employer who may hire union members or nonmembers. However, the nonmember must join the union within a certain period of time.

Union membership requirements vary. Generally, though, you can join one only if you work for a business that has a labor contract with a union. A labor contract is an agreement between the employer and its employees. It results from negotiations

Six hundred feet (183 meters) below the surface of Manhattan Island in New York City, workers bore through solid rock as part of replacing the city's water pipes, a project due for completion in 2020.

between the employer and the union. If you get a job at such a business, you'll be covered by the agreement.

In some states, workers must join the appropriate union and pay dues as a condition of employment. Twenty-four other states have "right to work" laws that allow workers to benefit from union-obtained wages and work conditions without being part of the union. According to the National Right to Work Legal Defense Foundation, in 2014 the following twenty-four states or territories had right-to-work laws: Alabama, Arizona, Arkansas, Florida, Georgia, Guam, Idaho, Indiana, Iowa, Kansas, Louisiana,

PLUMBERS LOCAL NUMBER 1

Plumbers Local Number 1 formed on April 18, 1854, when a group of journeyman plumbers in New York City officially adopted a constitution and by-laws. The group, which included workers from Brooklyn, Williamsburg, and Jersey City, had previously organized as a "protective society" called the Journeymen Plumbers Society. The group formed branches called locals in Brooklyn, New York City, and elsewhere.

The society also started two national pipe trades organizations that laid the foundation for national unionism in the pipe trades. Plumbing projects in New York City had existed as early as the mid-1700s. But it was the completion of the Croton Aqueduct System in 1842 that increased job opportunities for plumbers. The aqueduct was built to fight fires, but it also provided a way to pipe running water into buildings.

Demand for indoor plumbing exploded, and many new plumbing businesses formed. Some called themselves master plumbers and hired journeymen in the plumbing trade. The master plumbers formed a Master Plumbers Society. Its purpose was to control prices and standardize work

(CONTINUED ON THE NEXT PAGE)

(CONTINUED FROM THE PREVIOUS PAGE)

weeks and wages. Journeymen plumbers started their own group.

Thirty-five years later on October 11, 1889, the Brooklyn journeymen's local became Local Number 1 of the new United Association of Journeymen Plumbers, Gas Fitters, Steam Fitters and Steam Fitters' Helpers of the United States and Canada.

Today, the newly named United Association of Journeymen and Apprentices of the Plumbing and Pipe Fitting Industry of the United States, Canada (UA) represents approximately 340,000 plumbers, pipefitters, sprinklerfitters, service technicians, and welders in local unions across North America. It also complies with agreements of the Australian Plumbing Trades Employees Union and the Irish Technical, Engineering Electrical Union.

Michigan, Mississippi, Nevada, North Carolina, North Dakota, Oklahoma, South Carolina, South Dakota, Tennessee, Texas, Utah, Virginia, and Wyoming. In addition, the state of Colorado had a law with right-to-work provisions but that also allowed union-only employers if employees wanted a closed shop. Many unions and labor activists encourage workers to press for union membership and against right-to-work legislation because it is often seen as a way to bleed the labor movement of money by right-wing politicians and business interests.

PROS AND CONS

According to the US Bureau of Labor Statistics, in 2014 a higher percentage of plumbers, pipefitters, and steamfitters belonged to a union than the percentage in all occupations. The largest organizer of these workers is the UA.

Benefits of union membership generally include higher wages and benefits than would be enjoyed without the collective bargaining unions engage in. According to the most recent figures from the US Bureau of Labor Statistics, in 2010 unionized workers earned nearly 14 percent more than nonunion workers.

Such advantages as holiday pay, time off allowances, and worker safety provisions have resulted from union negotiations. So have medical benefits and premium payments. According to the National Compensation Survey by the US Bureau of Labor Statistics, 93 percent of union workers had health care benefits compared to 69 percent of nonunion workers. Unmarried domestic partners are more likely to have these benefits if their partner belongs to a union.

Union members also benefit from union advocacy in the workplace. If a member is treated unfairly, the union can intervene. It may actually determine disciplinary action and decide whether the worker can be fired. Unions also determine seniority rules for promotions and layoffs. Union membership might be a negative for some workers who do not want to be forced to join one or pay its dues.

And while unions have rules to ensure job security, especially for workers with seniority, the rules may limit promotion opportunities for more recent hires. The same goes for situations where layoffs must occur. Most often the rule is "last hired, first fired." Younger workers might sometimes be at a disadvantage. Union workers lose some of their individuality because majority rules on such issues as whether to strike. A member must accept whatever the majority decides whether he or she agrees.

JOB PROSPECTS

The outlook for workers seeking employment as plumbers, pipefitters, and steamfitters is good. Job opportunities will result from several factors. Over the next ten years, many of these tradesmen will retire, leaving a gap to be filled by younger workers. Competition for the jobs will not be as strong as in some times in the past. In fact, employers are reporting difficulty finding skilled workers for openings they already have.

These trades are somewhat sensitive to economic changes. Times of low growth may see reduction in the number of construction jobs for homes and other buildings. However, the need for maintenance and repair of plumbing and pipe systems offer these trades some job stability. So do stricter plumbing efficiency standards, the need to retrofit power plants, and changes in building codes for fire suppression systems. With competitive pay and strong market demand, a career as a plumber, pipefitter, or steamfitter is a good choice for hands-on, motivated, smart workers.

⌀ **What they do:** Plumbers, pipefitters, and steamfitters install and repair pipe systems for homes, businesses, and factories. The pipes carry gas, water, and other liquids to and from the structures, as well as within them.

⌀ **Work environment:** Most plumbers and fitters work full time, and overtime is common. They are often on call on nights and weekends to handle emergencies. These trades have among the highest rates of illness and injury compared with all occupations.

⌀ **Education and training:** These trades are usually licensed by the states with various education and training requirements. These generally include a minimum age of eighteen, a high school diploma or equivalent, classroom education from unions or technical schools, and paid, on-the-job training.

⌀ **Earnings:** Master plumbers and fitters earnings are about 20 percent higher than the median average for all construction trades and 30 percent more than the median average for all occupations.

⌀ **Job outlook:** Employment of plumbers, pipefitters, and steamfitters is projected to grow 12 percent from 2014 to 2024, faster than the average for all occupations.

GLOSSARY

agency shop An employer that uses the union as its bargaining agent, and all employees pay dues to the union even if they are not union members.

anaerobic bacteria Bacteria that grow without a need for oxygen.

brazing Soldering that uses an alloy of copper and zinc at a high temperature.

building codes Regulations or ordinances enacted and enforced by state and local governments that establish minimum standards to ensure structural safety of homes and other buildings.

closed shop A company that hires only union members in good standing.

deductive reasoning A way of thinking that applies general rules to specific situations.

fittings Such parts as joints, couplings, elbows, tees, or other connectors used to join pipes together.

gray water Household wastewater from showers, bathtubs, washing machines, and sinks.

groundwater Water that starts as rain or snowmelt and seeps beneath Earth's surface and collects in spaces between rock.

helper A building trades worker who assists plumbers, pipefitters, and steamfitters by doing lesser-skilled tasks than the qualified skilled workers.

HVAC The abbreviation for heating, ventilation, and air-conditioning systems.

hydronics A type of heating or cooling technology that transfers heat using water, vapor, or other fluid in a closed pipe system.

inductive reasoning A method of thinking that creates general rules by combining pieces of information.

labor contract An agreement between an employer and its employees that results from negotiations over wages, working conditions, benefits, and other issues.

labor union An organization of wage earners or salaried employees in a particular trade. The union seeks to protect and further such members' rights and interests as wages, benefits, and working conditions.

median average income The point where 50 percent of workers earn more and 50 percent earn less.

open shop (sometimes called a merit shop) A workplace that is free to hire both union members and nonmembers. Some open shops recognize the union as its only negotiating agent.

résumé A document that summarizes a candidate's education, qualifications, and personal and professional experience.

septic system A method that uses a tank and tank lines to treat and dispose of human sanitary waste.

solder An alloy—usually of tin and lead—that melts at a low temperature.

threading A way of assembling pipe systems using screw ends.

union shop An employer who may hire union members or nonmembers. However, the nonmembers must join the union within a certain period of time.

welding A method of joining metal pipes and parts together by heating them to the melting point using a blowtorch or other tools and then pressing or hammering them.

American Backflow Prevention Association
342 N. Main Street, Suite 301
West Hartford, CT 06117
(877) 227-2127
Website: http://www.abpa.org
The American Backflow Prevention Association is a nonprofit
    organization dedicated to keep drinking water safe from
    contamination. It provides education and technical
    assistance to its network of regions and chapters.

American Society of Plumbing Engineers (ASPE)
6400 Shafer Court, Suite 350
Rosemont, IL 60018-4914
(847) 296-0002
Website: https://www.aspe.org
Facebook: @AmericanSocietyofPlumbingEngineers
Twitter: @ASPE.org
The American Society of Plumbing Engineers (ASPE) is an
    international organization dedicated to advancing the
    plumbing engineering profession. It seeks to assist in the
    professional growth of its members and protect the health,
    welfare, and safety of the public.

American Society of Sanitary Engineering (ASSE)
    International
18927 Hickory Creek Drive, Suite 220
Mokena, Illinois 60448
(708) 995-3019
Website: http://www.asse-plumbing.org

Facebook: @ASSE1906

Twitter: @ASSE_Intl

ASSE's motto, "Prevention Rather than Cure," defines
its mission to improve the performance and safety
of plumbing systems via training and pushing for
improvements in the industry.

American Supply Association (ASA)

1200 North Arlington Heights Road, Suite 150

Itasca, Illinois 60143

(630) 467-0000

Website: http://www.asa.net

The American Supply Association (ASA) serves wholesaler-
distributors in the plumbing-heating-cooling-piping
(PHCP) and industrial pipe valve fitting (PVF) industries.
It encourages employee training and networking.

International Association of Plumbing and Mechanical
Officials (IAPMO)

4755 E. Philadelphia Street

Ontario, CA 91761

(909) 472-4100

Website: http://www.iapmo.org

Facebook: @IAPMO

The International Association of Plumbing and Mechanical
Officials assists code development and provides
education and product testing to protect public
health. It developed the Uniform Plumbing Code and
Uniform Mechanical Code.

International Code Council
500 New Jersey Avenue NW, 6th Floor
Washington, DC 20001
(888) 422-7233
Website: http://www.iccsafe.org
Facebook: @InternationalCodeCouncil
Twitter: @IntlCodeCouncil
The International Code Council develops model codes and
    standards for safe, sustainable, and affordable structures,
    including building safety and fire prevention codes.

NSF International
PO Box 130140
789 North Dixboro Road
Ann Arbor, MI 48105
(800) 673-3275
Website: http://www.nsf.org
Facebook and Twitter: @NSFIntl
Formerly known as the National Sanitation Foundation,
    NSF International seeks to protect and improve human
    health by creating standards and certifications to protect
    water, consumer products, and more. It tests and certifies
    products and provides education and risk management.

Plumbing Manufacturers International (PMI)
1921 Rohlwing Road, Unit G
Rolling Meadows, IL 60008
(847) 481-5500
Website: http://www.safeplumbing.org

Facebook and Twitter: @SafePlumbing
Plumbing Manufacturers International (PMI) advocates for
    water-efficient and safe industry products.

United Association
Three Park Place
Annapolis, MD 21401
(410) 269-2000
Website: http://www.ua.org
Facebook: @UnitedAssociation
Twitter: @UAPipeTrades
The United Association of Journeymen and Apprentices of
    the Plumbing and Pipe Fitting Industry of the United
    States and Canada represents plumbers, pipefitters,
    sprinklerfitters, service technicians, and welders in local
    unions across North America.

United Association Canada
442 Gilmour Street
Ottawa, ON K2P 0R8
Canada
Website: http://www.uacanada.ca
Facebook: @uacanadamembers
Twitter: @uacanada
Instagram: @ua.canada
Founded in 1889, United Association Canada is a trade union
    that represents three hundred thousand plumbers and
    fitters in Canada.

Blankenbaker, E. Keith. *Modern Plumbing*. Tinley Park, IL: Goodheart-Willcox, 2014.

Cool Spring Press Editors. *Black & Decker The Complete Guide to Plumbing*. Minneapolis, MN: Cool Springs Press, 2015.

Cory, Steve. *Plumbing*. Newtown, CT: The Taunton Press, 2017.

Lusted, Marcia Amidon. *Working as a Plumber in Your Community* (Careers in Your Community). New York, NY: Rosen Young Adult, 2015.

Nixon, James. *Plumber* (What We Do), London, UK: Franklin Watts, 2014.

Prestly, Donald R. *Plumbing Do-It-Yourself for Dummies*. Hoboken, NJ: Wiley Publishing, 2007.

Rose, Simon. *Plumber* (Dirty Jobs). New York, NY: AV² by Weigl, 2015.

Rudman, Jack. *Pipefitter: Test Preparation Study Guide*. Syosset, NY: National Learning Corporation, 2014.

Rudman, Jack. *Plumber: Test Preparation Study Guide*. Syosset, NY: National Learning Corporation, 2014.

Rudman, Jack. *Steam Fitter: Test Preparation Study Guide*. Syosset, NY: National Learning Corporation, 2016.

Rudman, Jack. *Steam Fitter's Helper: Test Preparation Study Guide*. Syosset, NY: National Learning Corporation, 2014.

Schneirov, Richard. *Pride and Solidarity: A History of the Plumbers and Pipefitters of Columbus, Ohio*, 1889–1989. Ithaca, NY: ILR Press Books, 1993.

Doyle, Alison. "Plumber Resume Sample." Balance.com,
September 4, 2017. https://www.thebalance.com
/plumber-resume-sample-2063584.

Egg, Jay. "Ten Myths About Geothermal Heating
and Cooling." EggGeothermal.com, September
17, 2013. http://energyblog.nationalgeographic
.com/2013/09/17/10-myths-about-geothermal-heating
-and-cooling.

Elejalde-Ruiz, Alexia. "Women in Trades Make Good Money,
but Getting in Can be Tough." *Chicago Tribune*, May 14,
2015. http://www.chicagotribune.com/business/ct
-women-in-trades-0417-biz-20150420-story.html.

"How To Become a Plumber: A Step By Step Guide to a
Plumbing Career." PlumbingApprenticeshipsHQ
.com. Retrieved October 3, 2017. http://www
.plumbingapprenticeshipshq.com/how-to-become-a
-plumber.

Knowles, Francine. "Women at Work: Plumbers a Rare Breed,
One Told 'Not What Girls Do.'" *Chicago Sun-Times*, June
24, 2016. https://chicago.suntimes.com/news/women-at
-work-plumbers-a-rare-breed-one-told-not-what-girls-do.

"Local 1 History." UA Local 1. Retrieved September 25,
2017. http://www.ualocal1.org/history.aspx.

Lusted, Marcia Amidon. *Working as a Plumber in Your
Community*. New York, NY: Rosen Publishing, 2015.

Mader, Robert. "Stop Calling Yourself a 'Plumbette.'"
Contractor, February 9, 2015. http://www.contractormag
.com/blog/stop-calling-yourself-plumbette.

"Not All Flushes Are Equal." Mr. Rooter.com, March 23,
2015. https://www.mrrooter.com/greater-syracuse/about

-us/blog/2015/march/not-all-flushes-are-equal-how-to -maintain-your-s.

O-Net Online. "Summary Report for: 47-2152.01—Pipe Fitters and Steamfitters." August 1, 2017. https://www .onetonline.org/link/summary/47-2152.01.

ThePlumber.com. "World Toilet Day 2016." Retrieved September 25, 2017. http://theplumber.com/world-toilet -day-2016.

SkillsUSA.org. "Why Career & Technical Education?" Retrieved October 2, 2017. https://www.skillsusa.org /about/why-career-technical-education.

Sokanu.com. "What Does a Pipefitter Do?" Retrieved September 29, 2017. https://www.sokanu.com/careers /pipefitter"What Does a Plumber Do?" Learn.org.

Tate, Kat. "What Do Gas Fitters Do?" Home Improvement Pages.com, April 19, 2013. https://www .homeimprovementpages.com.au/article/what_do _gas_fitters_do.http://learn.org/articles/What_Does_a _Plumber_Do.html.

US Bureau of Labor Statistics, US Department of Labor, *Occupational Outlook Handbook*, 2016–17 Edition, "Plumbers, Pipefitters, and Steamfitters." December 17, 2015. https://www.bls.gov/ooh/construction-and -extraction/plumbers-pipefitters-and-steamfitters.htm.

WiseGeek.com. "What Does a Sprinklerfitter Do?" Retrieved September 30, 2017. http://www.wisegeek.com/what -does-a-sprinkler-fitter-do.htm.

ABOUT THE AUTHOR

Mary-Lane Kamberg is a professional writer and author of such career titles from Rosen Publishing as *A Great Career as a Sports Agent; A Career as a Network Administrator; A Career as a Database Administrator; Getting a Job in the IT Industry; Working as a Mechanic in Your Community; Getting a Job in Law Enforcement, Security, and Corrections*; and *A Career as an Athletic Trainer*. She lives in Olathe, Kansas.

PHOTO CREDITS

Cover, p. 3 sturti/E+/Getty Images; pp. 6–7 JGI/Tom Grill /Getty Images; p. 10 JoAnn Snover/Shutterstock.com; p. 12, ©iStockphoto .com/monkeybusinessimages; p. 15 Peathegee Inc/Blend Images /Getty Images; p. 19 © iStockphoto.com/EyeJoy; p. 21 Jupiterimages /Pixland/Thinkstock; p. 25 Cameron Spencer/Getty Images; p. 27 Yurich /Shutterstock.com; p. 28 © iStockphoto.com/matrixnis; p. 33 Monty Rakusen/Cultura/Getty Images; p. 35 © iStockphoto.com/ DGLimages; p. 37 © iStockphoto.com/AlexRaths; p. 42 ALPA PROD /Shutterstock.com; p. 45 Highwaystarz-Photography/iStock/Thinkstock; p. 47 Andrey_Popov/Shutterstock.com; p. 49 Kathy Hutchins /Shutterstock.com; p. 51 Marilyn Angel Wynn/Nativestock /Getty Images; p. 53 Roy Mehta/Iconica/Getty Images; p. 54 mathisworks /DigitalVision Vectors/Getty Images; p. 59 Aisyaqilumaranas /Shutterstock.com; p. 62 Robert A. Sabo/Getty Images; interior pages background (pipes) StylePein/Shutterstock.com.

Design: Nelson Sá; Layout: Nicole Russo-Duca; Editor: Phil Wolny; Photo Researcher: Ellina Litmanovich